Collaboration

We dedicate this effort to our fellow collaborators,
those we know and those we have yet to meet.

Bob,
it takes one
to know all!

best,
Trina

ISBN: 978-1-105-60302-0

CONTENTS

This little book is a reminder that every day, almost every interaction provides opportunities for working with others to serve a collective purpose (whatever it may be). The glue that binds together all successful endeavors is a product of collaboration: the intentional process of honoring and encouraging one another's contributions in the pursuit of a common goal. Something that important should be at the forefront of all our minds, but the attributes of collaboration are seldom discussed, and seldom practiced well.

Why is this?

Having wrestled with these questions, we've come upon some possible answers. For starters, most of us imagine that we already know what collaboration is – and we assume we are good at it. Closer examination suggests that neither is true. We have all gathered insights from our experience, but rarely do we share them productively with our professional partners. Although we do acknowledge the need for collaboration, we don't often foster it intentionally, and when it does happen, we find it uncomfortable. True collaboration is something to which we all aspire, but seldom embody.

Many professionals have written books on this topic before. They talk about collaboration to inspire innovation, to promote a social cause, or to save a failing marriage. They tell you how to use collaboration in specific ways to accomplish something important. This text, however, tries to uncover the fundamentals of simply working together effectively and discusses the essential nature of successful, collaborative relationships.

Collaboration matters

The need for collaboration is everywhere. We often don't see how it shapes our lives, on a global scale and in our most intimate interactions. The challenges we face today and tomorrow demand that more people work together more effectively than ever before. We are guests on a vast interconnected world spinning through space. One small change at the everyday level can resonate across the entire planet. We are confronted by the need to engage our most vexing challenges and sparking opportunities the best way possible – together.

We hope this book will illuminate what we need to know, and how we can help each other achieve the boundless potential of conscious and concerted collaboration. This book is intended to raise questions about the value of collaboration – not necessarily to answer them.

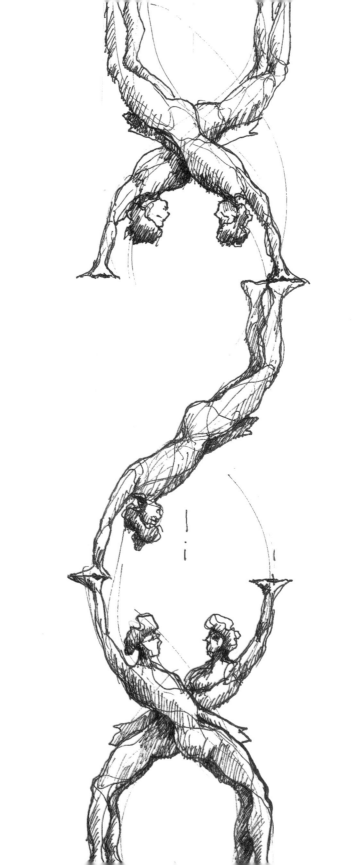

THE DNA OF COLLABORATION

It is important to know where we begin when we invoke the word 'collaboration.' Not surprisingly, the concept has a troubled past. The following is not intended to be a complete list of the core attributes of collaboration, but rather a simple beginning:

Definitions

The English collaborate comes from the Latin *collaborare*, meaning, simply enough, to work together. But during World War II, in the context of Vichy France, collaboration became a euphemism for traitorous cooperation with an occupying enemy. Consider The Times of London, 5 June 1943:

Not all have a record as black as Laval's ...
There were some who collaborated with a sick heart.

Collaboration's cousin, conspire, stems from the French *conspirer* – to breathe in unison – and means to harmonize, agree, or unite for a purpose. But since the late 14th century, the notion of working together has been overshadowed by dark speculations. To conspire was often 'to agree to do something criminal, illegal, or reprehensible together.' These connotations have been commonly invoked up to the present day in the term 'conspiracy theory', with its nefarious undertones.

We even have laws prohibiting collaboration. The legal definition of 'unlawful assembly' sends collaborators to jail in many countries, including the United States. California's Penal Code 407 prohibits the coming together of two or more people 'to do an unlawful act, or to do a lawful act in a violent, boisterous, or tumultuous manner.' In other words, we may be loud alone, but should collaborate quietly. In India, Section 144 of the Criminal Code prohibits assembly of four or more persons, along with public meetings. (That fourth collaborator seems to push things over the edge).

Shared experiences

Yet common ground is where collaboration takes root. Simply gathering together in the same place constitutes an important beginning: to establish a common ground ensures that a process is shared. But this is easier said than done. We forget that we share the profound human experiences of joy, sorrow, discovery, and creativity. These sympathetic life experiences should count for a lot, but they often do not get factored into our professional interactions. These commonalities lie hidden beneath our perceived differences in background, our divergent objectives, and our varied vocabularies. Fortunately, with a little effort, these points of reference can be uncovered.

We need to actively develop pathways to our commonalities. When a collaborative group eats together, visits a new place, or even watches a film, the new context relaxes the meeting-table roles we play and can open up collaboration in all its unpredictable manifestations.

Trust

Trust is the foundation for everything collaborative. We know that a great range of influences contributes to the establishment of trust. Other factors erode trust, such as preconceived ideas about what can and cannot be achieved, judgments about the abilities of others, suspicions about the purpose of the project, and more. We all bring so much baggage into the room – and we haven't even started! The fate of the collaboration seems to have been decided long before the meeting has begun. That is why concern, suspicion and unspoken criticism must be articulated and resolved at the outset. To do this is to affirm the terms of an honest enterprise, a trustworthy exchange. It includes every individual and their point of departure. Confidence in the process begins here, and it will flourish if openly pursued.

Candor

Even where the collaborative spirit is abundant, the penetrating voice of candor is often silent. For many reasons, we don't often receive rigorous criticism from those knowledgeable enough to provide it. Many do not want to speak out of turn, even when seniority and rank have been, in principle, checked at the door. As Richard Saul Wurman tells us "Stop saying 'uh-huh' when you don't know. Ask questions." But it is up to the leadership to grant permission to ask challenging questions, to offer incentives that turn candor into a prerequisite. To succeed, we must be able to both invite and sustain the honesty our work demands.

Humor

Perhaps the most obvious attribute of a successful collaborative group is that they laugh together. There is a chicken-and-egg thing going on here. Is it humor that opens people up, or openness that allows us to laugh? However it happens, humor is something to be encouraged. We are nourished by the levity of our collaborative conspirators as we engage the imperatives of our work. When the conversation turns contentious, we need to find perspective; what better vantage point than our good humor? A good friend once remarked that 'whimsy is the most powerful force in the universe.' Invite it in.

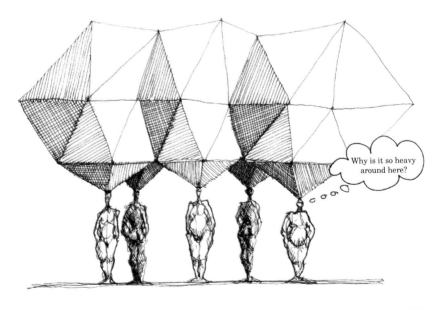

Every

needs

horse

project

come

lazy

Inclusion

Collaboration is neither democracy nor Utopia.
Not everyone gets invited to the party. To avoid
alienating potential partners, the suggestion here
would be to err on the side of inclusion. We can
tip our hat to Lyndon Johnson, who shrewdly
included J. Edgar Hoover in the creation of the

Civil Rights Act of 1964, noting that he would rather have him inside the tent pissing out, than outside the tent pissing in. Adversarial elements can threaten a collaborative project; best to keep them above ground and accounted for.

Participation

Woody Allen said that '80% of success is just showing up.' This holds for collaboration, too, as long as each participant 'shows up' fully. It is the reality that attendance in body alone can be worse than being present but disengaged. When participants are watching the clock, checking their phones, or being generally unresponsive, they can sap the energy of any collective effort. Often, we begin with the wrong question: We ask, 'What should I do?' when we might ask, 'How can I participate?' This second question speaks to the process of engagement rather than to a task to be completed. When we embrace deeper involvement, we immediately enter a realm larger than our individual contribution. We are nourished, and in turn we nourish other.

Conditioned Response

Of course it is not easy to participate. We can thank years of educational conditioning for the whispers in our ears: "You don't know enough to make a serious contribution. Watch and wait." If we do participate, we may do so hesitantly, imagining that what we have to offer is somehow inappropriate, that it lacks the magic ingredients of the 'right' answer or the 'informed' suggestion. Ken Robinson, a recognized leader in the development of education, reminds us that when children enter kindergarten, 90% of them consider themselves creative problem solvers. By the time they graduate from high school, only 12% do. What happened? Did they lose their creativity, or just their confidence?

The Group Genius

For some, collaboration is not a deliberate choice;
it is a way of solving problems that is deeply
interwoven into the communal experience.
In an attempt to measure individual
intelligence through a series of non-
verbal puzzles, it has been rumored
that anthropologists asked a group of
aboriginal people to assemble a pile of
interconnected blocks as quickly
as possible.
When the signal was given, they
converged around the first pile and
put it together in record time. Then they
went down the line together, pile by pile.
The anthropologists tried to explain that each
person needed to work independently,
but this rule was incomprehensible
to people who saw themselves as
inextricably connected to others in
pursuing a communal purpose.

The Lone Genius

Many of the signals we receive from an early age tell us to rely on our own resources – something about our 'bootstraps.' Our education system celebrates individual accomplishments, each of us wrestling with the material alone, barred from helping one another. The system offers little support for the collaborative spirit. We celebrate the role of the lone genius, the myth of the hero leader, the unique potency of the mad inventor.

Twenty-two versions of the incandescent lamp preceded Thomas Edison's and yet most Americans credit him with its 'invention.' As for the Wright Brothers, about twenty heavier-than-air mechanical flights had been documented prior to their first successful glider flight in 1902. By design or default, Edison and the Wrights were consummate collaborators who stood on the shoulders of many before them; how could they not be?

Yet the history books tell stories of brilliant, solitary minds – minds that we believe to be fundamentally different from our own. What if this isn't true?

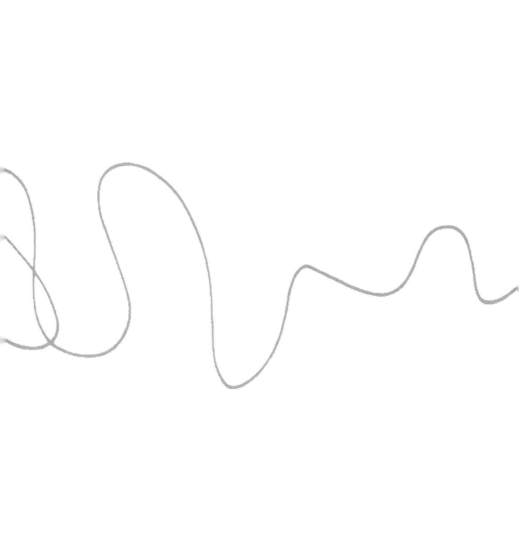

OBSTACLES

Many obstacles that prevent collaboration arise
from individual or societal bias. Many people seem
to think that each time we invite more voices into
the discussion, headaches multiply and results are
diluted. Too many cooks and that sort of thing. I have
heard otherwise reasonable friends and associates
say that collaboration is fine in principle, but in
practice it's no substitute for clear-headed leadership
and vision. This is true. Working collaboratively
is not a substitute for exercising leadership;
collaboration actually demands more from leaders
who employ it. The balance of imperatives against
the fluidity of the process can be daunting. In all
fairness, we all have some very good reasons to
sidestep collaborative opportunities. How would you
respond to the following comments?

I don't get it. Why are we ha
This is taking time away fr
what I really need to d
I want no part of a soon-to-be-failed experiment, done at the expense of my real work.
This project doesn't help me reach my goals, and I won't get credit for any of this.
If I wanted therapy, I'd go to a therapist.

I don't trust her motives. Her ego uses up all the oxygen in the room.
e all nodding... we don't agree.
If I say something, I might look uninformed... or worse.
Raise my hand? Not likely.

Obstacles: A coda

Most of us have had similar reactions at one time
or another in collaborative groups. Our robust egos
and societal inhibitors occasionally give way to the
call for collective action. It usually takes a crisis to
bring us together. Of course, crises abound, both big
and small. These inherent obstacles are not so easily
overcome, and this small book doesn't attempt to offer
a panacea. But the first important step is to know
that these obstacles exist, and they are formidable
opponents. Best to invite them into the tent.

wander
the edge
what yo

past
of
Knr

PATHWAYS TO SUCCESS

Listening

How do we practice something we think we already do well? Most of us assume we are communicating clearly all the time. The problem with our communication is that we are fulfilling only half of the bargain; we have so much to say that we forget to listen (or we're listening to ourselves). Yet, listening may be the most important element of collaboration. We credit ourselves with being attentive, but we recognize the real thing when we note: 'She's a good listener,' we inadvertently make an implicit confession; to listen well is rare.

The first step in listening well is simply to hear what someone is saying. The next step is to acknowledge what you 'think' you've heard, and not simply by nodding in agreement – that is diplomacy. Echoing back to the speaker what you have understood reinforces the authenticity of the interaction and may clarify the message for others in the room. To listen effectively is to reflect just enough comprehension back to the speaker while devoting your attention to what is being said.

From the other side, to be listened to, fully and earnestly, is to be accepted. Real listening encourages and supports a deeper, mutual exchange. Of course, being heard is so unusual and so unexpected that it can also be uncomfortable. As mild panic settles in, we admonish ourselves: 'Best say something useful!'

Opening the Door

Collaboration opens the door for more to enter. Inviting collaboration start with the basics; hearing everyone introducing themselves. Further devices can be used to open things up. For example each participant might pin a thought, concern, or revelation anonymously to the wall. Barriers break down and people get more comfortable with one another. Later, each participant might put forward an alternative to the plan being discussed, or suggest three good reasons why a popular idea is mistaken.

Finding strengths and weaknesses becomes the shared work. Issuing an invitation to participate fully makes it possible to explore, weight, and compare without injuring anyone's self-esteem. The discussion becomes livelier, the results richer.

Useful Conflict

Now that the doors are open, we need to be prepared
for whatever walks through – the good, the bad,
the ugly … and it can get ugly. But that's
okay, because conflict is both
unavoidable and essential in the
context of collaboration.
Until we push up against
one another, until an
earnest proposal meets
an equally earnest
rebuttal, we may be
getting along, but we
don't know quite where
we stand. Conflict can open
a conversation about a fuller
spectrum of possibilities.
The acceptance of conflict
demands openness.
Openness brings candor,
candor brings conflict
and conflict signals that
the collaboration is real. The
problem is that conflict can remain under the radar,
hidden in hallway conversations or whispered asides.
Best to have it out in the open where it can be useful.

46

The Utility of Failure

Wrestling matches like this mean that ideas get pushed, tested, and strained. Failure results. The gurus of collaboration – like IDEO designer Tim Brown and education guru Ken Robinson – urge us to 'fail early, and fail often.' Those most statistically successful collaborators – kindergartners – do not focus on failure at all. Their trials and errors are instead a seamless part of discovery (otherwise known as play). This works superbly for a short while until our parents, our educational system, and society at large indoctrinate us with definitions of right and wrong. Since acknowledgement of failure is a catalyst for any collaborative effort, pushing back against these powerful frameworks, while difficult, is essential to successful collaboration. We must accept inevitability of failure in order to transcend it. For those working alone, failure can be paralyzing. Members of a healthy collaborative group can insulate each other from fears that accompany failure. Nobody gets fired. All boats fall and rise with the tide.

Shared Aims

Collaboration requires a common aim – a direction
– distinct from the tactical goals that support it.
This defines a 'page' that everyone can turn to at
the outset, the choirmaster's C note that precedes
the singing of the choir. Rather than restricting the
conversation, a clearly articulated, shared aim, in
fact, allows for more creative digression, offering
wider insight and re-framing participation that may
have appeared irrelevant.

The adoption of a shared aim carries with it
a requirement: giving each participant a specific
assignment. In sport, knowing your position and
playing it promotes teamwork. The larger goal is to
defeat the other team, but each player has different
functions to perform to achieve it.

Improvisation

In the collaborative setting, people feel most comfortable when they know what their roles are and then use them as points of departure for lively, innovative play. The shared aim also allows for creative transcendence of 'position' to generate unexpected combinations and creative results. Without a starting position, new alignments and combinations are not possible. We do not know where collaborative forces will lead. The unexpected strengths and interactions of the participants create endless possible outcomes that can't be foreseen. Likewise, in jazz, an accepted tune or musical structure opens to tremendous freedom of expression in and around the implied form. The tune may never even be played ... yet it remains present, the parent of delightful, improvisational offspring.

Tethered Digression

With improvisation comes digression. Not all digressions are created equal, since not every side trip is tethered to a common aim or 'tune.' So often in a meeting, a wave of frustration rolls over us as someone wanders off the path of conversation. 'Stick to the point!' we silently shout. It is true. Staying with the topic is essential to pushing things to a conclusion. Yet tethered digression may allow collaborators to discover useful territory that would have otherwise been overlooked. Creative collaboration must harness the forces of inevitable wandering and targeted 'inefficiency.'

While the straight path marches towards the obvious horizon, divergence can broaden the field of vision. Meanwhile, it is not easy to pay attention when our fellow collaborators veer away from what we have been thinking. This again requires us to listen actively. As trust and familiarity and shared experiences accumulate, collaborators begin to trust 'divergent' detours and learn when and where to look for the 'convergent' pathways that allows a group to move forward.

Explore

the process

INCENTIVES

Collaboration demands extra time, money, patience, and energy. Is it worth it? Is it a luxury or a necessity? Are we wasting time or (ultimately) saving it? Is a collaborative effort the best response or a shallow compromise?

As long as participants view collaboration as an indulgence, they will gravitate toward the straightest path to completion. This will certainly yield a solution, but not necessarily the best one. For any collective effort that will require widespread support in the future, shortchanging the collaborative process could prove detrimental. The group may find itself reworking and backtracking in pursuit of consensus. This costs time and money. It is better to embrace the collaborative process from the beginning and get it right the first time.

When collaboration works, the results tend to be quietly durable, the conclusions balanced and robust. When collaboration is absent, the results can be disastrous. Like it or not, we are increasingly, inextricably connected to these disasters.

A Flood of Confusion

On Sunday, August 25, 2005, Hurricane Katrina reached Category 4 intensity, with winds gusting to over 215 mph. In so many ways, the federal, state and city governments were unprepared for the disaster that followed. Worse, the official response was slow, uncoordinated, inefficient and ineffective. The heroes who emerged were the first responders. Their stories of creative collaboration contrasted sharply with those in positions of governmental authority, whose lack of coordinated efforts seriously delayed rescue initiatives. A striking example was the initial refusal and late acceptance of international assistance by the U.S. government. There are, of course, complex institutional and bureaucratic impediments to what might have been a more collaborative response. At the same time, we see the need for both individual and organizational collaboration as we prepare for and deal with the environmental shifts that are occurring more often.

Deep Trouble

The Gulf Coast disaster provides a persuasive
example of the enormous costs of weak collaboration.
We do not have to look far to see the complexity
and depth of our self-generated local and global
problems: they monopolize the news. The British
Petroleum Deepwater Horizon oil spill in the Gulf
of Mexico that flowed for three months in 2010 was
the largest accidental marine oil spill in the history

of the petroleum industry. For weeks, we collectively fell into the growing gap between our actual and imagined capabilities. We saw how we are inextricably connected to these failures of collaboration, how our fates are intertwined, and how we must meet these challenges together. If we believe the illusion that BP must solve its own problems alone, then we multiply the collective costs and undershoot collective potentials, and by wide margins. The BP spill left 4.9 million barrels of crude oil in a 580-square-mile section of the Gulf. Its effects will be felt for decades. Would the costs have been different in an environment that valued openness and collaboration?

Mining the Possibilities

There are, near at hand, instructive examples of our own potential to collaborate. The 2010 Chilean mining accident began when a collapse trapped thirty-three men 2,300 feet underground, where they survived for a record 69 days. Once they found the miners alive, the government took over the rescue from Compañía Minera San Esteban, a company notorious for its unsafe mines. Chilean authorities deployed three large drilling rig teams, nearly every government ministry, and sought the expertise of NASA along with that of more than a dozen international corporations.

Foreman Luis Urzúa's levelheadedness and humor was instrumental in keeping the miners focused on survival. He credited the majority decision-making techniques employed in the collapsed tunnel for the positive esprit de corps and the group's dedication to a common goal. 'Everything was voted on. ...We were 33 men, so 16 plus one was a majority.' Did the collaborative actions of these desperate men waste time, or buy it?

False Security

Are the rest of us really so different? Look at
Fukashima's Tepco nuclear reactor meltdown. Many
concerns had been raised about plant safety in Japan,
and many inspection reports had been falsified.
The conversation about nuclear power was highly
constrained and hierarchical...and it resulted in a
massive gamble. A Japanese calamity becomes a
global calamity. We are all starting to look a bit like
miner; we are stuck, the familiar tools and remedies
no longer available. Someone said that there are no
natural disasters, just natural events with dire human
consequences. If every disaster is man-made, perhaps
by working together, some of them might be un-made.

NEW DIRECTIONS

While creating this book we often felt like
we were stating the obvious – and we
are. It feels obvious because we think we
know how to collaborate, though we may
have forgotten a few details. We think we
collaborate all the time – and tell ourselves
(and everyone else) that we do it so well. But
the way we actually work tells a different tale.
You might recall the parable of the blind men
and the elephant. A group of blind men encounter
an elephant and describe it very differently. Each
experiences something completely unique – a
tree trunk, a snake, a gurgling ocean, a rope –
and a few were wildly poetic, beyond what
anyone might see. In sum, their limited
observations yielded a more complete picture

of what was there, but without a collaborative lens to focus these impressions into a coherent whole, we are lost in the dark. If we do not make a concerted effort to share our perspectives, our world will be (like that of the blind men) small, subjective and incomplete.

We each have much to give. True collaboration creates the territory in which our individual talents, ideas and energy harmonize with those of the wider community. Every voice has something to add, but you must speak to be heard. Collaboration is extraordinary when we participate knowingly and whole-heartedly, calling upon every resource. By sounding such a simple note, we hope to resonate with others who suspect that it is more fun, and often more beautiful to play together. Thank you for playing!

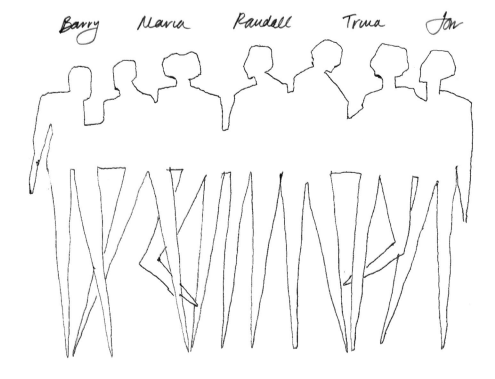

ACKNOWLEDGEMENTS

Any book on collaboration should have a broad base
of contributors, and this one surely does. The order
and the degree of participation is less important
than simply the fact that so many offered to play so
willingly. That in itself was a lesson in collaboration.
The idea of the book emerged from a wonderful
collaboration with Trina Learned, who lured me
into a presentation at the national convention of
the Society of College and University Planners. Our
topic was the process of campus planning, something
we felt we understood, but it evolved into a wider
embrace of what it actually means to work together,
something we realized was more elusive. The success
of that event prompted us to imagine that a wider
audience might appreciate a little book on the
topic. Trina spearheaded the initial effort, to which

most of our office contributed. The book, however, clearly required another level of involvement. Enter Maria Verrier and Jon Calame. What transpired was a gradual evolution of the most blissful working relationship I have ever experienced. Text, inspiration and insights were freely offered, and they each modeled at every turn the ideals of what a true collaboration might be. In this unique friendship, authorship is irrelevant, and while we decided that a single name is typically required on the cover, I feared we would be contributing to the myth of the lone creator.

Many friends and colleagues also gave freely of their time to contribute stories and observations about the nature of working together. Although these stories have not specifically appeared in the book, they are woven into the essence of it, and they were much appreciated. Along the way and most assuredly at the finale, we had the creativity and editing talents of Randall Hoyt, graphic designer and long-time conspirator on other projects. His rigorous reading of the last drafts improved them immeasurably. His design and editorial instincts have brought the book to life.

We had the benefit of many books previously written on this topic. A partial bibliography is provided simply to offer some of the sources of our inspiration. Although as far as we know he has never written explicitly about collaboration, we must mention the name of Sir Ken Robinson. His ideas, spirit and delightful humor came into our conversations so often; we could not fail to include him.

Lastly, I want to acknowledge the patient forbearance of my partners at our architectural practice of Svigals + Partners, Jay Brotman and Bob Skolozdra, who took up the slack as I engaged in what was not immediately contributing to our bottom line. They believe as I do in the profound necessity to work and play together. In the spirit of collaboration, we are all thankful.

Barry Svigals, FAIA
Svigals + Partners, New Haven, CT

BIBLIOGRAPHY

Bennis, Warren and Patricia Ward Biederman. *Organizing Genius The Secrets of Creative Collaboration.* New York: Basic Books, 1997.

Robinson, Ken, "Schools Kill Creativity." TED Conference. Feb. 2006.

Robinson, Ken, "Changing Education Paradigms." RSA Animate. Oct. 2012.

Sawyer, Keith. *Group Genius The Creative Power of Collaboration.* New York: Basic Books, 2007.

Winer, Michael and Karen Ray. Collaboration *Handbook Creating, Sustaining and Enjoying the Journey.* Saint Paul, MN: Fieldstone Alliance, 1994.

COLOPHON

This book was set in the typeface New Century
Schoolbook. The designer Morris Benton of American
Type Founders researched the subjects of eyesight
and legibility, then created Century Schoolbook, which
was released between 1918 and 1921. The Century
typefaces are still seen in elementary school texts, and
are noted for their exceptional legibility, so much so
that the Supreme Court of the United States requires
their briefs be typeset in them. Matthew Carter
developed the digital version of this earnest and
highly-functional typeface.

16411537R10048

Made in the USA
Lexington, KY
23 July 2012